Pocket Edition 100 FACTS
SHARKS

Pocket Edition 100 FACTS

SHARKS

Steve Parker

Consultant: Trevor Day

Miles Kelly

First published in 2005 by Miles Kelly Publishing Ltd
Harding's Barn, Bardfield End Green, Thaxted, Essex, CM6 3PX, UK

This edition updated 2014, published 2018

2 4 6 8 10 9 7 5 3 1

Publishing Director Belinda Gallagher
Creative Director Jo Cowan
Managing Editor Rosie Neave
Senior Editor Claire Philip
Designers Andrea Slane, Rob Hale
Cover Designer Simon Lee
Image Manager Liberty Newton
Indexer Jane Parker
Production Elizabeth Collins, Caroline Kelly
Reprographics Stephan Davis, Jennifer Cozens, Thom Allaway
Assets Lorraine King

ISBN 978-1-78617-622-6

Printed in China

British Library Cataloguing-in-Publication Data
A catalogue record for this book is available from the British Library

ACKNOWLEDGEMENTS

The publishers would like to thank the following sources for the use of their photographs:
t = top, b = bottom, l = left, r = right, c = centre

Cover: (front) Daniel Selmeczi/stevebloom.com, (back) A Cotton Photo/Shutterstock.com
Alamy 11 Zuma Press, Inc.; 32(b) Brandon Cole Marine Photography; 46–47 Reinhard Dirscherl
Ardea 45(tc) Valerie Taylor **Dreamstime.com** 13 Naluphoto **FLPA** 18–19 Stephen Belcher/Minden Pictures;
46(bl) Biosphoto, Jeffrey Rotman/Biosphoto **National Geographic Creative** 23(t) & 38 Jim Abernathy; 43 Paul
Sutherland; 45 Brian J. Skerry **Naturepl.com** 6–7, 14 & 35(t) Doug Perrine; 26–27 Bruce Rasner/Rotman;
28(b) David Fleetham; 35(cr) Georgette Douwma; 37(t) Alex Mustard Photoshot.com 15; 40
Oceans Image Science Photo Library 8–9 Andy Murch/Visuals Unlimited, inc; 10–11 Jaime Chirinos;
29(bx) David Fleetham, Visuals Unlimited; 36(t) Andy Murch /Visuals Unlimited, inc. Sea Pics 21(cr) Hirose,
(b) Espen Rekdal **Shutterstock.com** 2–3 frantisekhojdysz, 12(b) cbpix; 14(tr) Greg Amptman;
15(t) A Cotton Photo; 16–17 Rich Carey; 17(b) NatalieJean; 19(cl) BW Folsom; 19(br) cdelacy; 21(tr) Sedin;
22(b) Greg Amptman; 23(b) cbpix; 24–25 Brandelet; 27 L.Watcharapol; 28(t) Krzysztof Odziomek; 30 Rich
Carey; 32(t) FAUP; 32 L. Watcharapol; 35(b) BMCL; 36(b) Christophe Rouziou; 37(b) cbpix; 38–39 Rich Carey;
38 & 39 FAUP; 41 iliuta goean; 42–43 tororo reaction; 44(b) Arend van der Walt, 44(tr) Alex Pix; 47 Ru Bai Le

All other photographs are from: digitalvision, Image State, PhotoDisc

The publishers would like to thank Stuart Jackson-Carter for the artwork he contributed to this book.

All other artwork from the Miles Kelly Artwork Bank

Every effort has been made to acknowledge the source and copyright holder of each picture.
Miles Kelly Publishing apologises for any unintentional errors or omissions.

Made with paper from a sustainable forest

www.mileskelly.net

The publishers would like to thank the Shark and Coral Conservation Trust (SCCT)
for their help in compiling this book.

Contents

Fantastic fish

1 Sharks are meat-eating fish, and nearly all of them live in the sea. Many are active hunters and chase after their prey. Some lie in wait to grab their victims. Other kinds are scavengers, feasting on the dead bodies of animals such as whales and seals.

◀ Grey reef sharks are often seen in groups around coral islands, especially at night when they are most active. They are curious sharks that often swim close to divers, and near the water's surface.

The biggest sharks

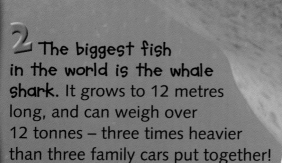

▶ The whale shark swims with its mouth wide open to filter krill from the water. Krill are usually 2 to 3 centimetres long. Millions of them, along with other small creatures, make up plankton.

2 **The biggest fish in the world is the whale shark.** It grows to 12 metres long, and can weigh over 12 tonnes – three times heavier than three family cars put together!

3 Whale sharks like cruising across the warm oceans. They swim up to 5000 kilometres in one year, but tend to visit the same areas at certain times of year, when their food is plentiful.

4 Despite the whale shark's huge size, it mostly eats tiny prey. It opens its enormous mouth, takes in a great gulp of water and squeezes it out through the gill slits on either side of its neck. Small animals such as krill and baby squid are trapped in the gills and then swallowed.

5 Whale sharks may sleep for weeks. It's thought that they sink to the seabed and lie there, hardly moving, for several weeks each year. This could help them to save energy when food is hard to come by.

▼ Ripple patterns on basking sharks are caused by sunlight shining through the waves onto the shark.

6 Basking sharks are huge! They are the second-biggest of all fish, reaching 10 metres in length and 6 tonnes in weight. Like whale sharks, basking sharks filter small animals and bits of food from the sea.

7 Some sharks like to eat stinking, rotting flesh! The Greenland shark can grow to a massive 7 metres in length. It feeds on all kinds of dead animal bodies, including whales, seals, dolphins, other sharks, squid and even drowned animals, such as reindeer.

▶ Greenland sharks rival great whites in size, weighing over one tonne. They swim slowly in the cold Arctic water.

9

Ancient sharks

▼ Sharks' basic body shapes and behaviour have hardly changed since they first appeared. The shark *Hybodus* lived about 160 million years ago in the Jurassic Period, during the Age of Dinosaurs.

8 **The first sharks lived more than 350 million years ago.** This was 120 million years before the dinosaurs lived on Earth. Dinosaurs died out around 65 million years ago but sharks survived. This means that sharks have ruled the seas for over twice as long as dinosaurs ruled the land!

▶ *Megalodon* was probably similar in appearance to today's great white. It was a top sea predator of its time and may have attacked marine mammals, such as this large whale.

9 **Some prehistoric fish are known as 'spiny sharks'.** This is because they had streamlined bodies like sharks, and sharp spikes on their fins and bellies. Their real name is acanthodians, and they lived in lakes and rivers 400 to 250 million years ago.

▲ A human diver looks tiny in comparison to the enormous *Megalodon* and its prey.

10 Some sharks are preserved in stone! Parts of sharks that died long ago have been preserved in rocks, as fossils. Most fossils are made of hard body parts, such as teeth and scales. The fossils show the size of the shark and even the kind of food it ate.

▶ Fossilized *Megalodon* teeth, being stone, are up to ten times heavier than they were in life.

11 The biggest shark in history was probably *Megalodon*. Its fossil teeth look like those of the great white shark, but they're twice as big. *Megalodon* could have been 15 or even 20 metres long – three times the size of today's great white. It lived about 20 to 2 million years ago and was a great hunter.

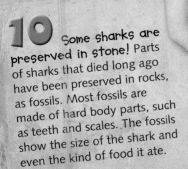

Megalodon

MAKE A MEGA MOUTH!

You will need:
black pen   big cardboard box   large pieces of white card   scissors   tape

1. Use the pen to draw a shark's mouth onto the box and cut it out.
2. Draw and cut out 20 teeth shapes from the white card.
3. Tape these inside the mouth. Draw on eyes. Now you can stare *Megalodon* in the face!

Super swimmers

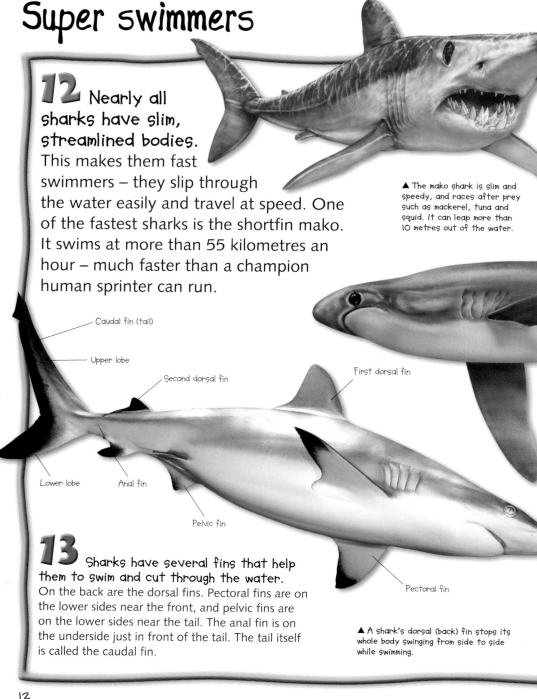

12 Nearly all sharks have slim, streamlined bodies. This makes them fast swimmers – they slip through the water easily and travel at speed. One of the fastest sharks is the shortfin mako. It swims at more than 55 kilometres an hour – much faster than a champion human sprinter can run.

▲ The mako shark is slim and speedy, and races after prey such as mackerel, tuna and squid. It can leap more than 10 metres out of the water.

Caudal fin (tail)

Upper lobe

Second dorsal fin

First dorsal fin

Lower lobe

Anal fin

Pelvic fin

Pectoral fin

13 Sharks have several fins that help them to swim and cut through the water. On the back are the dorsal fins. Pectoral fins are on the lower sides near the front, and pelvic fins are on the lower sides near the tail. The anal fin is on the underside just in front of the tail. The tail itself is called the caudal fin.

▲ A shark's dorsal (back) fin stops its whole body swinging from side to side while swimming.

14 Some sharks have tails longer than their bodies. The common thresher shark is 6 metres long – and half of this is its tail. The thresher uses it to attack smaller fish, so it can eat them.

▼ The thresher shark thrashes its tail from side to side to stun small fish before swallowing them.

15 Shark tails have other uses, too. Some sharks smack the water's surface with their tails to frighten their prey. Others swish away sand or mud on the seabed to reveal any hidden creatures.

BREATHING UNDERWATER

1. Most sharks have five pairs of gills
2. Fine blood vessels allow oxygen to pass from the water to the blood
3. Heart pumps blood around the body

▶ A shark's gill chambers are in its neck region. Most have five gill slits on either side.

16 Like other fish, sharks breathe underwater using their gills. These are under the slits on either side of the head, and are filled with blood. Water flows in through the shark's mouth, over the gills and out through the slits. The gills take in oxygen from the water because sharks need oxygen to survive.

17 Most sharks swim all of the time so that water flows over their gills and they can breathe. However some can lie still and make the water flow over their gills by 'pumping' the muscles of their mouth and neck.

Making a meal

I DON'T BELIEVE IT!
Tiger sharks have eaten all kinds of strange things – bottles, tools, car tyres, and in one case, a type of drum called a tom-tom!

18 Tiger sharks are famous for trying to eat almost everything! Some of the items they swallow are not even food for them. They have even been known to eat tin cans and shoes!

19 Many predatory sharks will eat any suitable fishy prey they come across. This includes smaller sharks of other species, as well as their own. They may even eat their young.

▲ Tiger sharks usually feed at night, preferring to hunt alone.

20 Tiger sharks swim right up to the beach. Most sharks stay away from the shore in case they get stranded and die. But tiger sharks will come near to the shore, especially at night, to explore for food.

◀ The tiger shark can swim in water so shallow that it would hardly cover your knees. Here it can catch animals such as baby seals, and seabirds like this young albatross.

21 Where there is sudden plentiful food, like a dead whale, sharks gather and seem to go crazy. They bite and snap at almost anything – and occasionally even nip each other. This is called a feeding frenzy.

◀ A feeding frenzy is more organized than it looks – sharks rarely injure each other.

22 Most sharks prefer just a few types of food. One kind of bullhead shark likes to eat only sea urchins. However, if it gets very hungry, it will try other foods.

23 Not all sharks have sharp, pointed teeth. The Port Jackson shark has wide back teeth, like rounded pebbles. It uses these to crush the hard body cases of its favourite food – shellfish.

▶ The Port Jackson shark's front teeth are small and pointy, the rear ones are broad and strong.

Shark bodies

QUIZ
Which of the following organs do both humans and sharks have in their bodies?
1. Stomach 2. Lungs
3. Spiral valve 4. Liver
5. Gills 6. Heart

Answers:
1, 4, 6

24 A shark has a skeleton but it is different to ours. The parts are made not of bone, but of a substance called cartilage. This substance is very strong and light, and also slightly bendy.

25 A shark's guts are about twice as long as its body. Swallowed food goes into the stomach, then along the intestine. This has a part called a spiral valve, found only in sharks and rays. It is shaped like a corkscrew and takes in nutrients from food.

Dorsal fin

Kidney

Intestines have a spiral valve

Backbone extends into tail

Stomach

26 Many sharks produce slime from their skin. It slides off the shark easily and helps the shark to swim faster. New slime is always being made quickly by the skin to replace the slime that flows away.

▲ The main parts of the skeleton are the skull, the ribs, the long backbone or vertebral column, and the fin spines.

27 Sharks have very tough skin covered with tiny, tooth-shaped points. These points are called denticles. In the bramble shark some of the denticles are much larger, forming sharp thorns and prickles for protection.

28 Shark skin can be useful. Through the ages it has been used by people as a strong material to make handbags, shoes, belts, cases, handle grips and even a special kind of sandpaper known as chagrin.

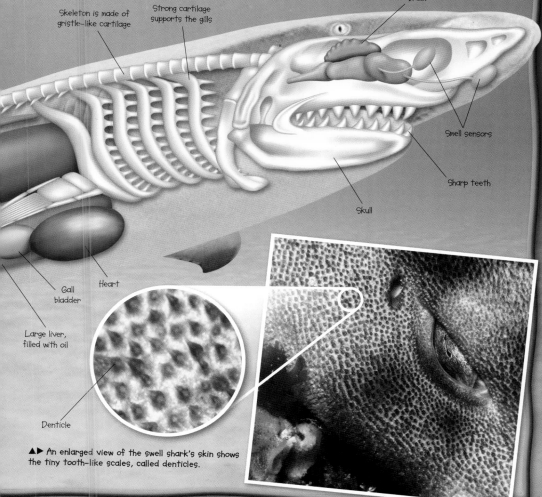

Skeleton is made of gristle-like cartilage

Strong cartilage supports the gills

Brain

Smell sensors

Sharp teeth

Skull

Gall bladder

Heart

Large liver, filled with oil

Denticle

▲▶ An enlarged view of the swell shark's skin shows the tiny tooth-like scales, called denticles.

Ultimate killer

29 The world's biggest hunting, or predatory, fish is the great white shark. It grows to 6 metres in length and can weigh more than one tonne. Great whites live around the world, mainly in warmer seas. They have a fearsome reputation.

▼ When attacking, the great white's final upwards rush, or charge, can carry it up to 5 metres above the surface.

30 The great white can raise its body temperature. It can make its body warmer than the surrounding water. This allows its muscles to work more quickly, so it can swim powerfully. It means the great white is partly warm-blooded, like humans.

31 Great whites let their victims bleed to death. They bite on their first charge then move off, leaving the victim with terrible wounds. When the injured prey is weak, the great white comes back to finish it off.

I DON'T BELIEVE IT!

A great white has about 300 razor-sharp teeth in its mouth. Its jaws open wide enough to swallow a whole seal in one gulp!

32 The teeth of the great white are up to 6 centimetres long. They are razor-sharp but slim, like blades, and they sometimes snap off. But new teeth are always growing just behind, ready to move forwards and replace the snapped-off teeth.

▼ The great white's upper teeth are triangular, the lower ones more pointed.

▼ Each tooth has jagged, saw-like edges called serrations.

34 The great white often attacks unseen from below. It surges up from the dark depths with tremendous power. It can smash into big prey such as a seal or a dolphin, and lift it right out of the water as it takes its first bite.

▶ When chasing prey or bait, great whites reach a top speed of over 40 kilometres an hour.

33 The great white 'saws' lumps from its victim. Each tooth has tiny sharp points along its edges. As the shark starts to feed, it bites hard and then shakes its head from side to side. The teeth work like rows of small saws to slice off a mouthful.

Strange sharks

35 **Six-gill sharks have an extra pair of gills.** This may be the number that ancient sharks had long ago. Six-gill sharks grow up to 5 metres long and eat various foods, from shellfish to dead dolphins.

Six pairs of curled gill slits

36 **Some sharks have frills.** The frilled shark has six pairs of wavy gill slits. It looks more like an eel than a shark, with a slim body 2 metres in length, and long frilly fins. It is dark brown in colour, lives in very deep waters and eats squid and octopus.

▲ Each tooth of the frilled shark has three needle-like points for grabbing soft-bodied prey.

▼ A saw shark may lose and re-grow as many as 30,000 teeth during its lifetime.

37 **The saw shark has a 'saw' for a nose.** Its long nose, or snout, is up to half its total length. The snout has teeth-like points sticking out from the sides. The shark uses its snout to dig around in sand and mud for prey.

38 The goblin shark looks
very strange! Few examples
have been found, so little is known
about its lifestyle. It swims in very deep waters
where there is no light – it may be able to
detect its prey using an electro-sense.

▲ This young goblin shark has not
yet grown its extra-long nose.

▼ The adult goblin shark's snout can be
one-quarter of its total length. The
jaws can move forwards, out of
the mouth, to grab small
fish and squid.

I DON'T BELIEVE IT!
The smallest sharks
could lie curled up in
your hand. The dwarf
lanternshark is just
20 centimetres
long!

39 Lanternsharks can
glow in the dark! They live in deep
dark water and have glowing spots on
their bodies, particularly around their
mouths and along their sides. The spots may
attract curious small creatures such as fish and
squid, so the shark can snap them up.

▶ The lanternshark's tiny
light-producing organs are
called photophores.

Amazing senses

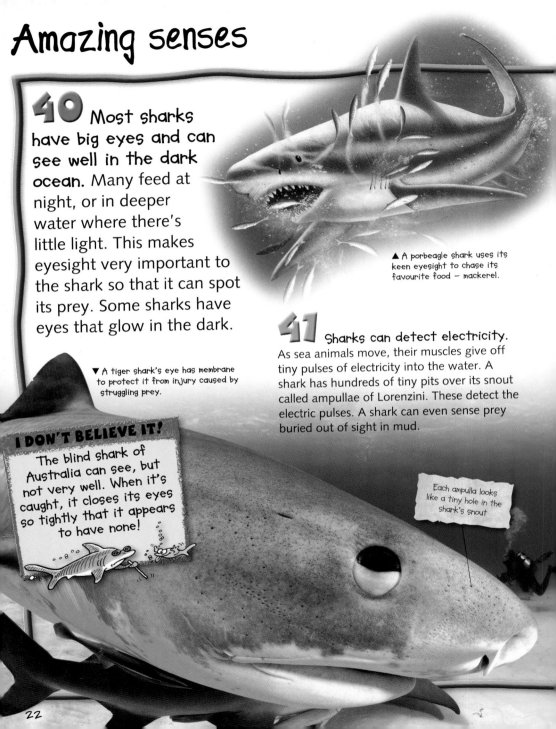

40 Most sharks have big eyes and can see well in the dark ocean. Many feed at night, or in deeper water where there's little light. This makes eyesight very important to the shark so that it can spot its prey. Some sharks have eyes that glow in the dark.

▲ A porbeagle shark uses its keen eyesight to chase its favourite food — mackerel.

▼ A tiger shark's eye has membrane to protect it from injury caused by struggling prey.

41 Sharks can detect electricity. As sea animals move, their muscles give off tiny pulses of electricity into the water. A shark has hundreds of tiny pits over its snout called ampullae of Lorenzini. These detect the electric pulses. A shark can even sense prey buried out of sight in mud.

I DON'T BELIEVE IT!

The blind shark of Australia can see, but not very well. When it's caught, it closes its eyes so tightly that it appears to have none!

Each ampulla looks like a tiny hole in the shark's snout

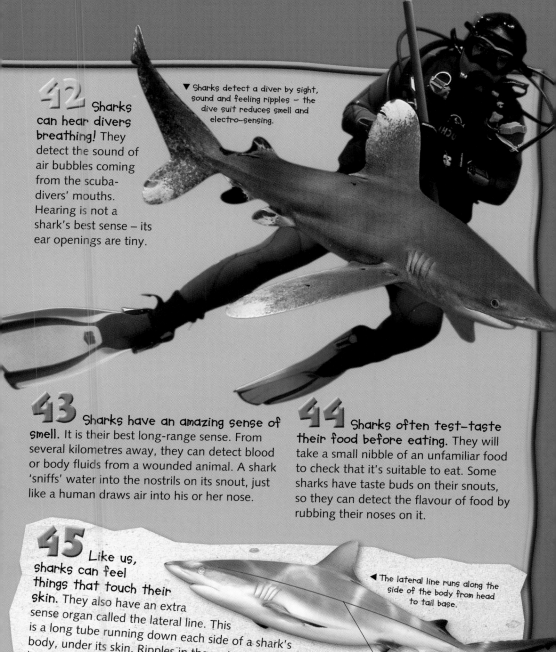

42 Sharks can hear divers breathing! They detect the sound of air bubbles coming from the scuba-divers' mouths. Hearing is not a shark's best sense – its ear openings are tiny.

▼ Sharks detect a diver by sight, sound and feeling ripples – the dive suit reduces smell and electro-sensing.

43 Sharks have an amazing sense of smell. It is their best long-range sense. From several kilometres away, they can detect blood or body fluids from a wounded animal. A shark 'sniffs' water into the nostrils on its snout, just like a human draws air into his or her nose.

44 Sharks often test-taste their food before eating. They will take a small nibble of an unfamiliar food to check that it's suitable to eat. Some sharks have taste buds on their snouts, so they can detect the flavour of food by rubbing their noses on it.

45 Like us, sharks can feel things that touch their skin. They also have an extra sense organ called the lateral line. This is a long tube running down each side of a shark's body, under its skin. Ripples in the water pass into the lateral line through tiny holes in the skin. Hairs inside the lateral line sense the ripples and send signals to the brain.

◀ The lateral line runs along the side of the body from head to tail base.

Lateral line

23

Hammers for heads

46 The hammerhead shark is named after the strange shape of its head. Experts suggest several reasons for this – one is that the head is shaped like the wings of a plane. As the shark swims, water flowing over its head helps to keep its front end lifted up, rather than nose-diving.

▶ The hammerhead's mouth is relatively small compared to the width of its head – but still deadly for small prey.

Large hammer-shaped head with eyes and nostrils at either end

Triangular, serrated teeth

47 The hammer-shaped head may improve the shark's senses. The nostrils are at each end of the 'hammer'. Smells drifting from the side reach one nostril well before the other. By swinging its head from side to side, the hammerhead can pinpoint the direction of a smell more quickly.

QUIZ

Why might hammerheads have hammer-shaped heads?

1. To break apart rocks to get at prey behind them.

2. To help sense the direction of smells in the water.

3. To smash open windows in shipwrecks.

Answer: 2

48 The great hammerhead is one of the biggest predatory sharks, growing to 6 metres long. There are another eight kinds of hammerhead shark, including the scalloped hammerhead and the bonnet-head.

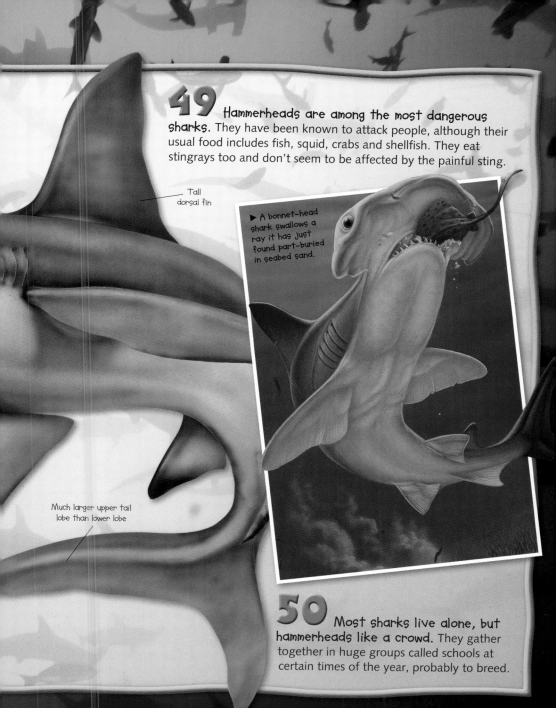

49

Hammerheads are among the most dangerous sharks. They have been known to attack people, although their usual food includes fish, squid, crabs and shellfish. They eat stingrays too and don't seem to be affected by the painful sting.

Tall dorsal fin

▶ A bonnet-head shark swallows a ray it has just found part-buried in seabed sand.

Much larger upper tail lobe than lower lobe

50

Most sharks live alone, but hammerheads like a crowd. They gather together in huge groups called schools at certain times of the year, probably to breed.

Big mouth

51 The megamouth shark was discovered in 1976 near Hawaii in the Pacific Ocean. An American research ship hauled in its parachute-like anchor to find a strange shark tangled in it.

▼ The megamouth's huge jaws are right at the front of its body, not slung under the head as in most sharks.

52 Megamouths open their mouths as they swim through shoals of krill. The prey get trapped inside the shark's mouth and then swallowed. The megamouth is not really an active hunter. It is a slow-swimming filter-feeder, like the whale and basking shark.

53 **Megamouths go up and down every day.** They rise near to the surface at dusk in order to feed during the night. At dawn they sink to deeper waters and spend the day in the dark, more than 200 metres down.

The loose skin and floppy fins show that the megamouth is a slow swimmer

54 **Megamouths are scattered around the world.** They have been caught in all the tropical oceans, especially in the Western Pacific and Indian oceans. Only about 50 have been found since its discovery. It may be that there have never been many megamouths in the world.

ARCTIC OCEAN

NORTH AMERICA

ATLANTIC OCEAN

EUROPE

ASIA

AFRICA

SOUTH AMERICA

PACIFIC OCEAN

INDIAN OCEAN

OCEANIA

SOUTHERN OCEAN

▲ Although the megamouth is rare, it can live worldwide. Each shark icon shows where a specimen has been found.

55 **The megamouth has a massive mouth more than 1.3 metres wide.** Its soft, flabby body is about 5 metres long. In the summer when it has been feeding well, it can weigh more than one tonne.

56 **Scientists believe that there may be more types of shark as yet undiscovered.** Sometimes the badly-rotted bodies of strange sharks are washed up onto beaches. But the remains are often too decayed to be identified.

Getting up close

▼ The whale shark has little to fear from humans, so divers can usually approach, and even grab a ride by holding the dorsal fin.

57 **Some small types of shark are fairly safe and people can swim near them with care.** In some tourist areas, people can even feed sharks. The sharks seem to become trained to accept food from divers.

58 **Some sharks, however, are dangerous to swim with.** Although the cookie-cutter shark is only 50 centimetres long, it has a large mouth and big, sharp teeth. This shark attacks targets much larger than itself, biting out small patches of skin and flesh, before racing away. It even snaps at humans – the first recorded case was in 2009. Victims are left with neat round holes in their bodies.

▶ The circular bite mark made by a cookie-cutter shark can be clearly seen on this spinner dolphin as it leaps through the waves.

QUIZ

Which sharks aren't
usually dangerous to people?

1. White-tip reef shark

2. Great white

3. Nurse shark

4. Thresher

5. Tiger shark

Answer:
1, 3, 4

59 Some sharks get used to
accepting food from people. This means
that they get out of the habit of hunting.
When the people are no longer around, the
sharks start to starve.

60 Feeding and
touching sharks is now banned in
some places. Sometimes a shark snatches
and swallows the food while it's still in a bag or net.
This could give the shark bad stomach-ache, or even kill it.
Also, touching sharks and other fish can damage their skin,
scales and layers of body slime.

▶ A shark cage allows
divers to get a close up
view of a great white. An
encounter like this would
be incredibly dangerous
without it.

29

In the family

61 Sharks have close relations that also have skeletons made of cartilage rather than bone. Other kinds of cartilaginous fish include skates and rays, and the chimaera.

▼ The huge manta ray has two fleshy 'lobes' on its head that guide water into its mouth. The manta then filters the water to find food.

62 Skates and rays are flat fish, but not flatfish. True flatfish, such as plaice, have bony skeletons and lie on their left or right side. Skates and rays have very wide bodies with flattened upper and lower surfaces, and long narrow tails.

THE FLYING RAY

You will need:
scissors   stiff paper   coloured pens
sticky tape   drinking straw
modelling clay

1. Cut out a ray shape from paper and colour it brightly. Fold it along the middle so the 'wings' angle upwards.
2. Stick the straw along the underside, so part sticks out as a 'tail'. Add a blob of modelling clay to one end.
3. Launch your 'flying ray' into the air. Adjust the tail weight until it glides smoothly.

63 A ray or skate 'flies' through the water. The sides of its body extend out like wings. The 'wings' push the water backwards, and so the ray or skate swims forwards. Unlike sharks and other fish, the ray's tail is rarely used for swimming.

64 **The biggest rays are mantas.**
They measure up to 7 metres across and
weigh nearly 2 tonnes. Manta rays have huge
mouths and feed like whale sharks by filtering
small creatures from the water. Despite their
great size, mantas can leap clear of the surface
and crash back with a huge splash.

▶ The blue-spotted
stingray grows to about
35 centimetres across.

65 **Stingrays have
sharp spines on their long
tails.** They use them like daggers
to jab poison into enemies or victims.
Some stingrays live in lakes and rivers.

Pale undersides
with blotches

Short tail
without sting

Large
pectoral fins

66 **Sawfish are different
from saw-sharks.** A sawfish is
shaped like a shark, but it is a
type of ray with a long snout
edged by pointed teeth. A
sawfish has gill slits on
the bottom of its
body, rather than
on the side.

Edged with sharp 'teeth'

Gilll slits

Long, saw-like
snout

▲ The sawfish uses its saw to catch prey,
either by swiping at shoals of fish, or
sifting through sand to find crustaceans.

Meeting and mating

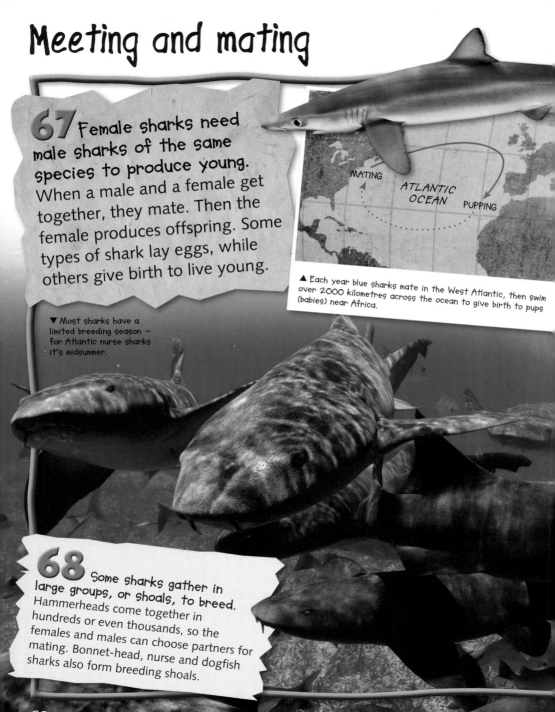

67 Female sharks need male sharks of the same species to produce young. When a male and a female get together, they mate. Then the female produces offspring. Some types of shark lay eggs, while others give birth to live young.

MATING

ATLANTIC OCEAN

PUPPING

▲ Each year blue sharks mate in the West Atlantic, then swim over 2000 kilometres across the ocean to give birth to pups (babies) near Africa.

▼ Most sharks have a limited breeding season — for Atlantic nurse sharks it's midsummer.

68 Some sharks gather in large groups, or shoals, to breed. Hammerheads come together in hundreds or even thousands, so the females and males can choose partners for mating. Bonnet-head, nurse and dogfish sharks also form breeding shoals.

▲ Male white-tip reef sharks rest in the shallows, waiting for scents called pheromones to drift through the water, which tells them that females are nearby.

69 Sharks have a complicated way of getting together. They give off scents into the water to attract a partner. Then the two rub one another, wind their bodies around each other, and sometimes even bite the other. The male may hold the female using his claspers, which are two long parts on his underside.

70 Some sharks don't breed very often. This can cause problems, especially when people catch too many of them. The sharks cannot breed fast enough to keep up their numbers, and they become rare.

Eggs and babies

71 **Some mother sharks lay eggs.** Each egg has a strong case with a developing baby shark, called an embryo, inside. The case has long threads, which stick to seaweed or rocks. Look out for empty egg cases on beaches. They are known as 'mermaids' purses'.

▼ A baby catshark develops slowly in its protective case. At 50 days it is smaller than its store of food, the yolk. It gradually develops and finally hatches eight months later.

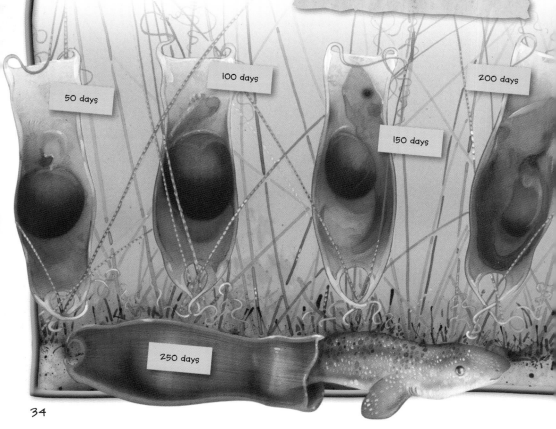

50 days

100 days

150 days

200 days

250 days

► Shark pups, like this newborn baby lemon shark, receive no parental care and must survive by themselves from birth.

72 Some mother sharks give birth to live baby sharks, known as pups. The basking and hammerhead shark do this. The pups have to look after themselves straight away.

▲ This just-hatched bamboo shark pup, about 30 centimetres long, still has some yolk as food.

73 Some sharks have hundreds of babies at once. The whale shark may give birth to as many as 300 pups, each about 60 centimetres long.

74 Many young sharks die. The mothers lay eggs or give birth in sheltered places such as bays, inlets and reefs, to try and keep the pups safe. But they are easy prey for hunters, such as dolphins, barracudas, sea lions and other sharks.

◄ The egg cases of the Port Jackson shark are spiral-shaped. The mother picks up each egg in her mouth and wedges it into a safe place, such as under a rock.

Hide and seek

75 Some sharks blend into their surroundings. This is called camouflage. The wobbegong has a lumpy body with blotches and frills that look just like rocks and seaweed. It waits for a fish to swim past, then opens its huge mouth to grab the victim.

▶ The mottled pattern, lumpy skin and frilly mouth of the wobbegong means it is difficult to spot from above, as it lies silently on the seabed.

76 A young zebra shark's stripes may camouflage it as it lies on ridges of mud or sand formed by water currents. The stripes also blend in with the shadows on the seabed formed by ripples on the surface above. As the shark grows, its stripes split into spots.

▼ This adult zebra shark's spots were once connected to form stripes.

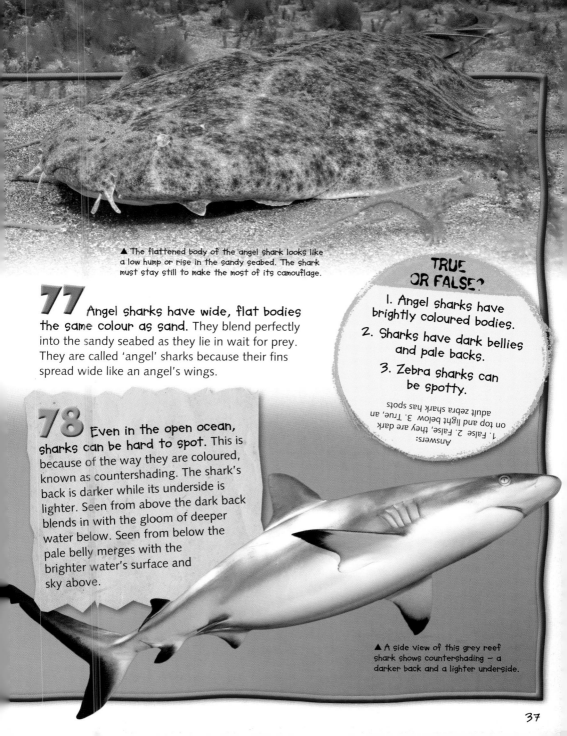

▲ The flattened body of the angel shark looks like a low hump or rise in the sandy seabed. The shark must stay still to make the most of its camouflage.

77 Angel sharks have wide, flat bodies the same colour as sand. They blend perfectly into the sandy seabed as they lie in wait for prey. They are called 'angel' sharks because their fins spread wide like an angel's wings.

78 Even in the open ocean, sharks can be hard to spot. This is because of the way they are coloured, known as countershading. The shark's back is darker while its underside is lighter. Seen from above the dark back blends in with the gloom of deeper water below. Seen from below the pale belly merges with the brighter water's surface and sky above.

▲ A side view of this grey reef shark shows countershading — a darker back and a lighter underside.

Making friends

79 Some fish enter a shark's mouth — and live! These small, brightly coloured fish are called cleaner wrasse. The shark allows them to nibble off bits of skin, scales and pests such as sea leeches and barnacles from its body, gills, mouth and teeth. The shark gets cleaned, and the cleaner fish have a good meal. This is an example of 'symbiosis'.

▼ This lemon shark is waiting patiently as striped cleaner wrasse move in between its teeth, cleaning as they go.

▼ Two remoras are attached to this bull shark, while another three swim alongside, ready to eat any leftovers.

80 Some fish attach themselves to sharks and travel with them through the ocean. Remoras, or sharksuckers, have a ridged sucker on their heads. This clamps to the underside of a large shark (or other big sea creature). The remora saves energy by getting a free ride, and it can let go to feed on the shark's scraps.

81 Pilotfish like to swim very close to sharks. They often cluster just below and in front of the shark's mouth. This may make them feel safe from large predators, and it allows them to catch bits of food falling from the shark's mouth. They may also be saving energy by swimming in the shark's slipstream – the swirls and currents made by its movement.

82 Some creatures that get close to sharks are not so friendly. Copepods, small crab-like creatures, will attach themselves to a shark's eyes, gills, snout or fins. They then nibble the shark's skin or even suck its blood.

◄ A pilotfish swims close underneath the mouth of a blue shark.

39

On the move

83 There are about 470 kinds of sharks, but only a few leave the sea and swim into the fresh water of rivers. One is the bull shark, which travels hundreds of kilometres up rivers, especially in South America.

84 Sharks may have a built-in compass. People use magnetic compasses to find their way across the seas or remote lands. The compass detects the natural magnetism of the Earth and points north-south. Sharks may be able to detect the Earth's magnetism too, using tiny parts of their bodies.

85 The most widespread sharks are blue sharks. They are found in almost every part of every ocean, except the icy polar seas. In the Atlantic Ocean, they travel from the Caribbean to Western Europe, down to Africa, and back to the Caribbean – 6000 kilometres in one year!

▶ Bull sharks have been known to attack people fishing, washing or boating in lakes. These bull sharks are in the Bahamas, very close to the shore.

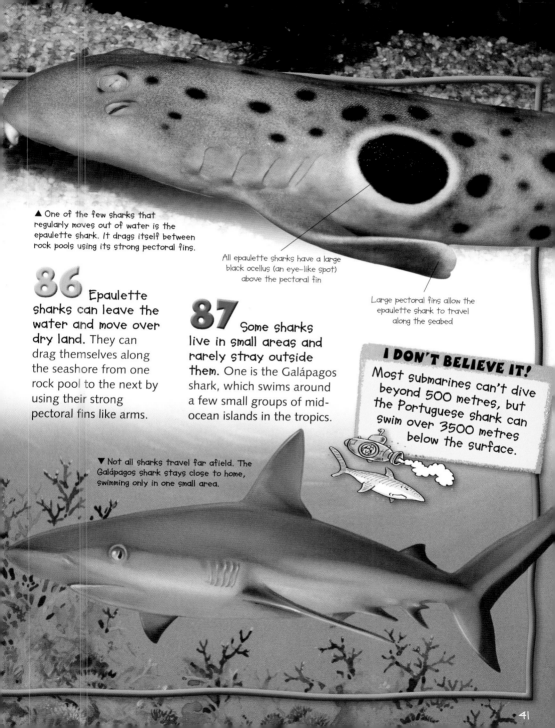

▲ One of the few sharks that regularly moves out of water is the epaulette shark. It drags itself between rock pools using its strong pectoral fins.

All epaulette sharks have a large black ocellus (an eye-like spot) above the pectoral fin

Large pectoral fins allow the epaulette shark to travel along the seabed

86 Epaulette sharks can leave the water and move over dry land. They can drag themselves along the seashore from one rock pool to the next by using their strong pectoral fins like arms.

87 Some sharks live in small areas and rarely stray outside them. One is the Galápagos shark, which swims around a few small groups of mid-ocean islands in the tropics.

I DON'T BELIEVE IT!

Most submarines can't dive beyond 500 metres, but the Portuguese shark can swim over 3500 metres below the surface.

▼ Not all sharks travel far afield. The Galápagos shark stays close to home, swimming only in one small area.

Science and sharks

88 Scientists study how sharks live, behave and travel. Small radio-transmitter trackers can be attached to big sharks and the radio signals show where the shark roams. Scientists attach little plastic tags with letters and numbers to the fins of smaller sharks. If the shark is caught again, its code can be traced.

89 Sharks show us problems in the oceans. In some areas, sharks have disappeared for no obvious reason. This might suggest chemicals and pollution in the water, which upset the balance of nature. The chemicals could affect the sharks themselves, making them unwell so that they travel away. Or the pollution could affect the sharks' prey, meaning they have to hunt elsewhere for food.

▶ Attaching a tracker or tag to a shark's dorsal fin takes just a few seconds.

90 Some shark species can live in captivity.

Sharks are popular with visitors to aquariums because people love to get up close. The sharks can also be studied to help us learn more about the species and how to protect them in their natural habitats.

▼ Huge aquariums let us watch the fascinating underwater world of sharks and other fish.

91 Sharks may help us to find new medicines.

Sharks seem to suffer from diseases and infections quite rarely compared to other animals. Scientists are examining their body parts, blood and the natural chemicals they produce in order to make better medical drugs for humans.

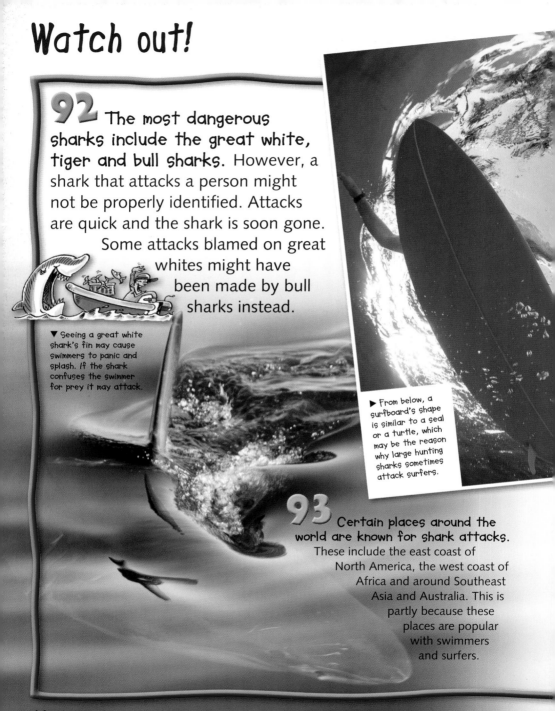

Watch out!

92 The most dangerous sharks include the great white, tiger and bull sharks. However, a shark that attacks a person might not be properly identified. Attacks are quick and the shark is soon gone. Some attacks blamed on great whites might have been made by bull sharks instead.

▼ Seeing a great white shark's fin may cause swimmers to panic and splash. If the shark confuses the swimmer for prey it may attack.

▶ From below, a surfboard's shape is similar to a seal or a turtle, which may be the reason why large hunting sharks sometimes attack surfers.

93 Certain places around the world are known for shark attacks. These include the east coast of North America, the west coast of Africa and around Southeast Asia and Australia. This is partly because these places are popular with swimmers and surfers.

▶ A chain-metal shark suit protects this diver as a blue shark 'mouths' or test-tastes.

94 Most shark attacks aren't fatal. A shark may 'test-bite' a person before realizing they aren't its normal prey. The victim may be injured, but not killed. Sharks will usually only attack people if they are hungry, or they may mistake humans for their normal prey.

▶ Safe from attack beyond the rope, tourists watch and learn as trained blacktip reef sharks are fed.

95 The dangers of shark attacks can be reduced in many ways. Examples include shark barriers or nets around the beach, patrols by boats and planes, lookout towers, and only swimming in protected areas.

96 Sharks are not the world's most dangerous animals. Each year, many more people are killed by poisonous snakes, tigers, elephants, hippos and crocodiles.

Save our sharks

QUIZ

Put these sharks in order of size, starting with the smallest to the biggest:

A. Great white

B. Lesser spotted dogfish

C. Nurse shark

D. Frilled shark

Answers:
1. B 2. D
3. C 4. A

97 **Some shark species have become very rare.** There are lots of reasons for this – pollution, hunting by people who think that all sharks are dangerous, sports angling where people use rods and lines to hook sharks, catching sharks for their meat, and catching sharks by accident in nets meant for other fish.

▼ By getting very close to sharks, and studying their behaviour, experts can help the conservation effort.

◄ Disguarded fishing nets can trap sharks, such as this young hammerhead.

98 **Live sharks can be worth more than dead ones.** People pay to see sharks in their natural habitats, viewing from glass-bottomed boats or underwater tunnels. In ecotourism, people experience nature without damaging it, and profits are used to help animals, plants and their habitats.

99 Sharks can be made into many foods, including shark fin soup. Many other shark parts are eaten or used by people around the world, including the flesh as shark steaks, and the liver and other body parts in various oils, cosmetics and health foods. Sometimes, it's not obvious because names are changed. Meat from a dogfish shark may be sold as 'rock salmon' or 'rock cod'.

▲ Shark oil is said to improve health, but there is no scientific proof.

100 Some sharks need our help, or they will die out forever. One of the best ways is to set aside huge areas of sea and coast as marine nature reserves or sanctuaries. Here all the animals can be protected from harm.

Index

Page numbers in **bold** refer to main entries, those in *italics* refer to illustrations